Addicts & Angels

Inspirational Quotes of A Soul's Guide to Recovery

Expanded Edition with
Journaling Section

JOHN CAMPBELL

Addicts & Angels – Inspirational Quotes of A Soul's Guide to Recovery
© John Campbell

First Edition published in 2025
Expanded Edition with Journaling Section published in 2025

ISBN: 978-1-0684132-5-4

Cover design: OnDesign South Africa
Interior design: IsaDesign.net

All rights reserved. No part of this book may be reproduced by any mechanical, photographic, or electronic process, or in the form of a phonographic recording; nor may it be stored in a retrieval system, transmitted, or otherwise be copied for public or private use—other than for "fair use" as brief quotations embodied in articles and reviews—without prior written permission of the publisher.

The author of this book does not offer medical or psychological advice, diagnose any physical, mental, or emotional condition, or recommend any particular treatment for any situation the reader wishes to address.

The author intends only to offer information of an anecdotal and general nature from his own experience and insights, to inspire the reader to make your own decisions to enhance the quality of your life. In the event you or others use any of the information or content in this book, you are fully responsible for your life path choices. The author and the publisher assume no responsibility for the direct or indirect consequences of choices you make.

This book is intended to encourage you to find well-being and success according to your own inner guidance and/or the support of qualified professionals of your choice.

Published by Wise Owl Secrets
Printed in United Kingdom

All quotes from A Course In Miracles, copyright ©1992, 1999, 2007 by the Foundation for Inner Peace, 448 Ignacio Blvd #306, CA 94949, www.acim.org and info@acim.org, are used with permission.

Also By John Campbell

Miracle Relationships

A Path to Freedom and Joy

First Published by O-Books, 2023 Copyright Statement
Copyright © 2025 by John Campbell

Contents

Foreword 6
Acknowledgements 8
Introduction 10

PART ONE 13

A Cry for Help 15
The Beginning of a New Life 17
Searching for Something More 19
Finding My Path with A Course in Miracles 20
An Invitation to You 22

PART TWO 25

QUOTES, POEMS, SONGS AND INSPIRATIONAL WRITINGS 27

My Introduction to Reading 30
The Family Afterwards 45
Uncovering the Fear 49
Everyone comes into your life for a reason, some for a season, and some for a lifetime 51
Understanding the Power of Acknowledging that I know nothing 54
The Power of Hugging 56
Who Am I? 59
Continuing the search for this thing called 'God' 63

Ask and You'll Receive 66
Early Childhood Programming 68
The Power of The Mind 73
Finding My Real Home 75
A Closing Reflection – A Message of Hope 82

Appendix 87

PERSONAL JOURNALING

Writing down your thoughts, insights, and inspirations can be a profoundly healing and empowering practice. To support you on your journey, I've included 100 additional blank pages at the end of this book for personal journaling. These pages offer space for reflection, self-inquiry, and integration of what you've read.

They are organised into five sections of 20 pages each:

- Pages 89–108 – Gratitude Journaling
- Pages 109–128 – Forgiveness List (Self & Others)
- Pages 129–148 – Unhelpful Beliefs to Release
- Pages 149–169 – New Empowering Beliefs to Embrace
- Pages 170–190 – Daily Affirmations

Feel free to use these sections as suggested, or in whatever way best serves your healing and growth.

Foreword

It is said, "Your most valuable gift to the world is your own story."

This is certainly true of John Campbell, whose journey from darkness to light is absolutely compelling. It is even more meaningful because it is not just John's story. We have all gotten lost in a far country, and we are finding our way home.

John's most powerful attribute is his sincerity. The depths of his heart touched the depths of mine. Those who encountered Jesus said that he was an unusual teacher because "he spoke with authority." Anyone who speaks truth from his soul shares that authority. John Campbell is such a one.

In this companion volume to the larger book, *Addicts and Angels – An Unusual Spiritual Journey*, John pinpoints the most poignant moments in his journey to recovery, and skillfully weaves them with the prose, poetry, and music that inspired him. Now we can all benefit from what benefitted John.

In mythologist Joseph Campbell's classic paradigm of The Hero's Journey, we learn that every person who takes the Great Adventure and captures the Holy Grail—a healing spiritual insight— must return to the world and share the gift with those on an earlier stage of the path. The book you are holding represents the spiritual hero disseminating the golden gifts that he has gleaned.

If you are open to receiving these gifts, your journey will be shorter and easier, your suffering lessened, and your joy expanded. John has trampled down some very tall weeds for us, that our road may become softer and wider.

At a time on the planet when fear, divisiveness, and insanity are rampant, anyone who progresses from pain to peace makes an unspeakably important contribution. I pray that John's awakening extends to you, and to those whom you love and touch.

This outstanding book is relatively short in length, but extremely long in power to heal. My deepest thanks to John Campbell for the extraordinary spiritual work he has done, the hurdles he has overcome, and the wisdom he has gained and now courageously shares.

Our lives are better for the transformation from addicts to angels, our own stories uplifted and blessed.

Alan Cohen

Acknowledgements

Expressing my gratitude is both a joyous and challenging task, as I would love to acknowledge every individual who has touched my life by name. While it's impossible to name everyone, I am comforted in the belief that they all know who they are.

I will, however, name and honour these organisations and people who have significantly supported my healing journey from self-loathing to self-love.

My path to first awakening began at *Broadway Lodge*, the treatment center I entered in 1997. To all the beautiful souls who guided me back to life, you are forever in my heart.

I extend heartfelt thanks to the friends I've made in *Alcoholics Anonymous* and to *Dr. Bob* and *Bill W.*, whose co-founding of this incredible movement has saved millions of lives in every corner of the world since 1935.

To the late *Bob Hoffman*, founder of *The Hoffman Process* in 1967, and to *Tim Laurence* and *Serena Gordon* for bringing this transformative work to the UK in 1995, along with all the dedicated teachers worldwide—this was a monumental step in my recovery.

In my quest for spiritual growth, I immersed myself in the writings of remarkable authors. My deepest gratitude goes to

Louise Hay, *Dr. Wayne Dyer*, *Dr. Deepak Chopra*, *Dr. Bruce Lipton*, *Joseph Murphy*, *Dr. Joe Dispenza*, *Tony Robbins*, and *Paul McKenna*. Special thanks to *Esther Hicks*, the late *Jerry Hicks*, and *Abraham* for the joy they've all brought to my journey.

After I discovered and eventually dedicated myself to practicing *A Course in Miracles*, many beautiful teachers and authors illuminated my path. I am grateful to the original founders of the *Foundation for Inner Peace*, *Dr. Helen Schucman*, *Dr. William Thetford*, *Dr. Kenneth Wapnick*, and *Judith Skutch Whitson*. My wife and I were fortunate to spend a day with Judy in her 89th year; her joy and youthful spirit exemplified the transformative power of living the Course's principles.

I would like to express my gratitude to the authors and teachers who have profoundly deepened my understanding of *A Course in Miracles*. They include *Alan Cohen*, *David Hoffmeister*, *Carol Howe*, *Gary Renard*, and *Robert Holden*. Each enriched my practical application of the Course, infusing it with the essential ingredients of a deep sense of humour—a quality I deeply enjoy. This resonates with one of the Course's pivotal teachings, reminding us that the separation began when *"the Son of God remembered not to laugh."*

I also wish to extend my appreciation to *Ian Patrick*, *Dan Strodl*, *Teresa Yiannaco*, *Sharon Scarth*, and all those who support the *Miracle Network in the UK*, with which I have been associated for over twenty years.

Finally, to all my beautiful family who have stood by me throughout this journey—my heart overflows with love and appreciation for each of you. Especially for your understanding of my love for my 'extended family' of the world.

Introduction

Hello, and welcome. My name is John Campbell, and I'm delighted to share this book with you. It is a companion to my autobiography, *Addicts & Angels: An Unusual Spiritual Journey*, and an invitation to explore some of the readings that inspired me on my journey of recovery and my search for God.

Addicts & Angels is my story. I call it a story because, as both a student and teacher of *A Course in Miracles*, I have come to understand that our physical lives are just that—a story, or rather, a dream. The purpose of this dream is to awaken from the illusion of who we think we are and discover who we truly are.

This story has everything—pain, suffering, shame, and guilt, but also redemption, joy, and, ultimately, real Divine love. It reveals the depths to which I fell as I tried to mask my pain and self-loathing with alcohol, hiding behind the carefully constructed façade of a successful man.

Alcohol is a powerful drug. It transformed me from a sensitive, shy young child into an adult desperately driven to succeed at all costs in search of approval. As my addiction progressed, my morals eroded, my self-worth crumbled, and my need for escape grew stronger.

I became trapped in a cycle of compulsive risk-taking, corporate fraud, and international oil and whisky smuggling. I am not proud of the depths to which I sank or the pain I caused my family and others. But I do know that I would never have committed those acts had my mind not been numbed by years of excessive alcohol abuse.

I believe that most crimes are committed under the influence of mood-altering substances. This is not to justify my own wrongdoing, or anyone else's, but to acknowledge that addiction often lies at the root of destructive actions. Eventually, alcohol stopped working for me. And when my pain became greater than my fear of change, I cried out for help.

PART ONE

A Cry for Help

In 1997, my life appeared to be falling apart. To the outside world, I had everything: a beautiful family, success, prestige as co-owner and Vice Chairman of *Brighton & Hove Albion FC*—my boyhood football club—and a luxury house in the Sussex countryside.

But behind closed doors, I was living a lie. Each night, I would return to that beautiful house, remove my camouflage—my suit, tie, waistcoat, and shiny shoes—and fall to my knees in prayer. My nightly plea was always the same:

"Please, God, don't let me wake up in the morning."

That was the moment I realised I had reached the end of the road. I needed help. I prayed again—this time, not to die, but for help to live.

Help arrived in an unexpected and miraculous way. An old friend and former drinking friend, whom I had lost touch with for years, contacted me out of the blue. After I opened up to him about my desperation, he encouraged me to call *Broadway Lodge*, a rehabilitation center in the Somerset town of Weston-Super-Mare, where he had received treatment for his alcoholism years before.

I made the call. That single act gave me my first glimmer of hope.

The Beginning of a New Life

Admitting myself to *Broadway Lodge* was the first step toward healing. I spent weeks in deep introspection, confronting the pain I had long tried to escape. It was there that my Spiritual Awakening—as I call it—truly began. I took my first tentative steps toward a more fulfilling and authentic life, eventually experiencing a sense of freedom and joy that I never imagined possible.

During my stay, I discovered a passion for literature. Books, poems, and articles that I once had no interest in now spoke to me in ways I couldn't ignore. They became a vital part of my recovery, offering inspiration and guidance. This newfound love of words also reawakened my own creative writing ability.

One particularly profound experience involved a poem my mother had written many years before. As a teenager, I had memorised it to gain her approval, but during a moment of meditation at *Broadway Lodge*—forty years later—the words resurfaced in my mind.

Her poem described a treatment center called *Laughton Hills*, where she had sought help for her own alcoholism. As I wrote the words down, I was struck by how closely her experience mirrored my own at *Broadway Lodge*. Inspired, I adapted her poem, weaving in my own experiences. I later shared my version, *Broadway Lodge*, with the counsellors. To this day, it still hangs on the wall in their office.

Searching for Something More

After completing my time in treatment, I spent years exploring different spiritual practices and healing courses. I knew I was searching for something—but I did not yet realise that something was God.

The great Sufi poet *Hafiz* once said:

> "In the end, we all only have two choices.
> We either come to God dressed for dancing,
> or we get wheeled into God's Ward on a stretcher."

I like to think I arrived somewhere in between—on walking sticks!

Eventually, my search led me to *A Course in Miracles.*

Finding My Path with A Course in Miracles

I first heard about *A Course in Miracles* in 2000 from a friend at college. I bought a copy of the book and dipped into it occasionally, but I struggled to understand its meaning. Even after attending study groups, it still felt out of reach.

Then I remembered an old saying:

"When the student is ready, the teacher appears."

I wasn't ready yet.

But in 2004, something changed. I received an unexpected email from *Dr. Wayne Dyer's* newsletter recommending a book called *The Disappearance of the Universe* by a new author, *Gary Renard.*

My intuition screamed at me: "This book is for you!"

I ordered a copy, and as soon as I started reading, I was captivated. The book explained the teachings of *A Course in Miracles* in a way that finally made sense to me. The wisdom and clarity were stunning.

From that moment on, I became a dedicated student of *A Course in Miracles*. I followed its early guidance—not worrying about fully understanding the text, but simply practicing the lessons. And as I did, my life transformed.

Now, I am committed to sharing this work with those people who come forward asking for more information. At last, I felt my search had ended.

This work, for me, ticked all the boxes. It explained the true purpose of my life. It made sense of everything.

An Invitation to You

Now, I invite you to explore some of the writings that inspired me throughout my journey—including my poem. These words carried me through the darkest times and into the light, and my hope is that they will inspire, comfort, and guide you on your own path.

This is not just a book of quotes. It is a reflection of my journey—what I call *Uncovery, Recovery, and Discovery.*

I trust that you will find wisdom in these pages, reassurance in the messages, and above all, inspiration to continue your own journey of healing and self-discovery.

PART TWO

QUOTES, POEMS, SONGS AND INSPIRATIONAL WRITINGS

1

Broadway Lodge

"This house, which stands upon the hill,
is peaceful and serene.
As I look from my bedroom, I behold a wondrous scene.
The daffodils, the rose beds, the rabbits in the fields,
and all the different fragrances which Mother Nature yields.

The morning air is mellow now,
the fruit upon the trees is ripening
and brings to me its scent upon the breeze.

I've traveled far, I've traveled wide,
I've sailed the mighty sea,
but never have I found such love
as Broadway shows to me.

And now I turn my thoughts toward
those gentle folk within,
for 'tis they who provide the loving care
which I have found therein."

I'd now like to share the words of a beautiful song by an American spiritual songwriter and singer called *Kirtana*. This is her song *Who You Really Are* from her album *This Embrace.*

I offer Kirtana my heartfelt thanks for all her magical work and for giving me her permission to reproduce these words for you.

2

Who You Really Are

by Kirtana

"Could there be more to this life we call mine
than a journey through space or a storyline,

more to life than the body can sense,
than the mind can conclude from experience?

Does who we are begin with breath,
depend on form or end with death?
Strip away these roles, these names,
and tell me what remains
and who you really are, who you really are.

We measure success by the things we accrue,
or the bonds that we form, or the deeds we do.
But these too shall pass,
as hard as we try to hold on to form, form will die,
but inherent in this dance of form
is the chance to see what's yet unborn,
and the choice to throw this chance away
and be caught up in the play
of who we think we are, who we think we are.

This is your lifetime. It could end at any time.
Where is your attention? Where is your prayer?
Where is your song?

In a fortunate life comes a call to be free
from the cycle of bondage and misidentity,
to wake from the dream and finally realise
the truth of one's being before the body dies.

So before the final scene is passed,
see the screen on which it's cast.
See what's seeing this me and you,
and then you'll see who you really are, who you really are."

My Introduction to Reading

"Once you learn to read, you will be forever free."

Frederick Douglass

It's an interesting fact that when I eventually admitted myself into this treatment center at the age of 51, I had not actually read anything substantial in my whole life.

I read my school study books and, of course, books to assist in my training to become a navigating officer and eventually a Captain in the Merchant Navy. But I had never read anything remotely spiritual.

However, we were all required to begin reading and studying a book called *Alcoholics Anonymous*, affectionately known as *The Big Book of AA*. This book truly inspired me and began my first understanding of this thing called 'alcoholism' and 'addiction'. From there, I started to read a lot more interesting spiritual books.

There were also certain writings which I had learned as a child that inspired me. I'd like to share the first one, which I learned off by heart and, later, encouraged my son to do the same. It is the famous poem *If* by *Rudyard Kipling*.

I was always drawn to this poem, partly because, like Kipling, I was also born in India, and I have always felt a deep connection to that country.

3

If

by Rudyard Kipling

"If you can keep your head when all about you
are losing theirs and blaming it on you.

If you can trust yourself when all men doubt you,
but make allowance for their doubting too.

If you can wait and not be tired by waiting,
or being lied about, don't deal in lies,
or being hated, but don't give way to hating,
and yet don't look too good nor talk too wise.

If you can dream and not make dreams your master.
If you can think and not make thoughts your aim.

If you can meet with triumph and disaster,
and treat those two impostors just the same.

If you can bear to hear the truth you've spoken
twisted by knaves to make a trap for fools,

or watch the things you gave your life to, broken,
and stoop and build them up with worn-out tools.

If you can make one heap of all your winnings
and risk it on one turn of pitch and toss
and lose, and start at your beginnings,
but never breathe one word about your loss.

If you can talk with crowds and keep your virtue,
or walk with kings, not lose the common touch.

If neither foe nor loving friend can hurt you,
if all men count with you, but none too much.

If you can fill the unforgiving minute
with sixty seconds' worth of distance run,
yours is the earth and everything that's in it,
and—which is more—you'll be a man, my son."

The next piece is also a very famous one, which contains so much wisdom that I've come to understand, and it's a favorite of many peoples, and it is

4

Desiderata

by Max Ehrmann

"Go placidly amid the noise and haste and
remember what peace there may be in silence.

As far as possible, without surrender,
be on good terms with all persons.
Speak your truth quietly and clearly and listen to others,
even the dull and ignorant.
They too have their story.

Avoid loud and aggressive persons.
They are vexatious to the Spirit.
If you compare yourself to others,
you may become vain and bitter,
for always, there will be greater
and lesser persons than yourself.

Enjoy your achievements as well as your plans.
Keep interested in your career, however humble;
it is a real possession in the changing fortunes of time.

Exercise caution in your business affairs,
for the world is full of trickery.
But let this not blind you to what virtue there is.
Many persons strive for high ideals,
and everywhere, life is full of heroism.

Be yourself. Do not feign affection,
neither be cynical about love,
for in the face of all aridity and disenchantment,
it is as perennial as the grass.

Take kindly the counsel of the years,
gracefully surrendering the things of youth.
Nurture the strength of spirit to shield
you in sudden misfortune,
but do not distress yourself with imaginings.
Many fears are born of fatigue and loneliness.

Beyond a wholesome discipline, be gentle with yourself.
You are a child of the universe,
no less than the trees and the stars.
You have a right to be here,
and whether or not it is clear to you,
no doubt the universe is unfolding as it should.

Therefore, be at peace with God,
whatever you conceive Him to be,
and whatever your labours and aspirations,
in the noisy confusion of life,
keep peace with your soul.

With all its shams, drudgery, and broken dreams,
it is still a beautiful world.
Be careful. Strive to be happy."

One of the things that I did while I was in the treatment center was to start attending church. A traditional Christian church local to the treatment center, where I would go every Sunday. At that early stage of my recovery, I was getting in touch with a lot of pain that I had suppressed and covered with years of alcohol abuse. I remember receiving a lot of comfort from attending these services on Sundays, especially from the hymns that were sung.

One of my favourite hymns at that time was *Amazing Grace*. Interestingly, I later discovered that the person who wrote this hymn, *John Newton*, was also an alcoholic sea captain involved in smuggling. So, we had something in common!

While my illicit cargoes were oil and whisky, he was smuggling human beings out of Africa and selling them in the slave trade in America. One day, while crossing the Atlantic, he had a spiritual awakening. He immediately turned his vessel around, went back to Africa, and set free the enslaved people he had captured.

He then returned to his native England and began his service to God, becoming a preacher. So here is his hymn.

5

Amazing Grace

by John Newton

"Amazing grace! How sweet the sound
that saved a wretch like me!
I once was lost, but now am found,
was blind, but now I see.

'Twas grace that taught my heart to fear,
and grace my fears relieved.
How precious did that grace appear
the hour I first believed!

The Lord hath promised good to me,
His word my hope secures.
He will my shield and comfort be
as long as life endures.

When we've been there ten thousand years,
bright shining as the sun,
we've no less days to sing God's praise
than when we first begun".

After getting sober, I was surprised by how much I cried.

Every time I attended church, as soon as the hymns began, I found myself sobbing. Whenever a counsellor or one of my peers paid me a heartfelt compliment, my eyes would well up with tears.

It took nearly a year before this habitual crying finally subsided. I had been carrying an immense amount of grief and loss, including witnessing some horrific accidents at sea resulting in the death of my shipmates. I had never allowed myself to acknowledge these feelings. As the Captain, I felt I had to stay strong and instead I buried them beneath years of excessive alcohol use, numbing myself to the pain.

Now in the safety of the treatment centre, at times, I felt disturbed and even embarrassed by how easily my emotions surfaced. But my counsellors saw it differently. They expressed appreciation and admiration for my willingness to be vulnerable. They reassured me that my openness was not a weakness but a strength—one that set a powerful example, especially for the other men in the group.

Many men are conditioned to believe that "real men don't cry." That belief runs deep, shaping how we express—or suppress—our emotions.

One day, a facilitator in our group played a song that spoke directly to this struggle. It was called *Real Men Cry*, written and performed by the gifted spiritual singer-songwriter *Karen Taylor Good*.

The song, co-written with her husband at the time, *Bill Taylor Sparks*, resonated deeply with me. Its message was one of healing—breaking free from old conditioning and embracing the truth that real strength lies in authenticity.

I am deeply grateful to Karen for granting me permission to share the lyrics of this beautiful song in this book.

6
Real Men Cry

by Karen Taylor Good

"I know that you've heard all your life:
emotions make men weak.
You must be brave, you must be bold,
and tears are for the meek.

And so you've held it all inside, like you were taught to do,
but your soul feels like it's dying. It's time to tell the truth.

Real men cry, real men feel,
real men are not - made of steel.
And real men hurt, in spite of what you've learned.
Believe me, it's no lie. REAL MEN CRY.

Forget what you were told to be, just be the things you are:
a man of passion, fire, and dreams, who listens to his heart.

A man who doesn't hide himself behind a wall of stone
and shows the world he's human,
made of tears and flesh and bone.

Real men cry, real men feel,
real men are not - made of steel.
And real men hurt, in spite of what you've learned.
Believe me, it's no lie. Real men cry.

After a lifetime of pretending,
what you knew was never true,
you can write a brand-new
story—it's time to be the real you.

Real men cry, real men feel,
real men are not made of steel.
And real men hurt, in spite of what you've learned.
Believe me, it's no lie. Real men cry."

One of the first things I had to learn in the treatment center was how to truly listen—because listening is an art. It's a real skill, and for someone as driven as I had become, it was a challenge.

I had been a leader from a very young age. By 26, I was the captain of my own ship, always in a position of authority. I expected people to listen to me, not the other way around. So learning to listen was a completely new experience—one that transformed the way I related to others.

In treatment, we did an exercise that was profoundly eye-opening. We were given the chance to experience both what it felt like to be truly listened to—and what it felt like not to be listened to. The difference was striking, and it taught me just how powerful deep, attentive listening can be.

Later, I came across a passage that beautifully captures the essence of real listening. It resonated deeply with me, reinforcing the idea that one of the greatest gifts we can offer—whether to our partners, friends, or anyone—is simply being fully present and listening.

7

How to Listen

Haleigh Lovell

'When I ask you to listen to me, and you start giving me advice, you have not done what I asked.

When I ask you to listen to me, and you begin to tell me
why I shouldn't feel that way,
you are trampling on my feelings.

When I ask you to listen to me and you feel you have to do something to solve my problem, you have failed me.

Strange as it may seem, listen: all I asked was that
you listen—not talk, not do—just hear me.

I can do for myself. I am not helpless.
Maybe discouraged and faltering, but not helpless.

And when you accept as a simple fact that
I do feel what I feel, no matter how irrational,
then I can quit trying to convince you
and get about the business of understanding
what's behind this irrational feeling.

When that is clear, the answers are obvious,
and I don't need advice.

Irrational feelings make sense when we
understand what's behind them.

Perhaps that's why contemplation works sometimes
for some people, because Great Spirit is mute.

It does not give advice or try to fix things.
It just listens and lets us work it out for ourselves.

So please listen and just hear me.

And if you want to talk, wait a minute
for your turn, and I'll listen.

Maybe if we both sit and listen to each other,
we'll be able to solve even greater problems than our own,
and perhaps we will even hear the mute
voice of Great Spirit".

After leaving my dangerous business behind, I found myself developing a deep interest in education—specifically, how we prepare children for adulthood.

Through a series of synchronistic events, which I describe in my book, I was guided to explore the education system more deeply. I felt certain there had to be a better way to equip children for life, one that nurtured their natural curiosity and confidence rather than suppressing it.

During my research, I came across a unique school on the east coast of England called *Summerhill.* This school had gained fame—and stirred controversy—for its unconventional, child-led approach to learning. Traditional educators considered its methods radical, and the school even had to fight legal battles in the British High Courts of Justice to protect its ethos. But it won.

Curious and inspired, I visited *Summerhill*, and what I saw was remarkable. Children were free to choose how they spent their time, engaging in what genuinely interested them. The result? A level of self-esteem and independence that was truly inspiring.

At some level, I must have always known this kind of approach was possible because I had been a free-spirited child myself. But formal schooling had always felt confusing and restrictive to me. Seeing *Summerhill* in action confirmed something I had long suspected—there is another way.

It reminded me of a profound passage from the great Chinese philosopher *Lao Tzu*, found in Chapter 57 of *The Tao Te Ching*.

8

If I Keep from Meddling

Lao Tzu

"If I keep from meddling with people,
they take care of themselves.
If I keep from commanding people,
they behave themselves.
If I keep from preaching at people,
they improve themselves.
If I keep from imposing on people,
they become themselves".

This simple philosophy struck me as profoundly true.

The next piece is a reflection on what happens when we break free from the systems that try to keep us small.

One of the most profound realisations I had on my journey was understanding that there is a part of me—and a part of everyone—that is unlimited.

This story, both playful and deeply insightful, beautifully illustrates that truth.

9

Chickens and Eagles

Adapted from Prince Ea's

The Eagle Story

"One day, a naturalist who was passing
by inquired of the owner why it was that an eagle,
the monarch of all birds, should be confined to live
in the barnyard with the chickens.

"Since I have given it chicken feed and trained it to be
a chicken, it has never learned to fly," replied the owner.

"It behaves as chickens behave, so it is no longer an eagle."

"Still," insisted the naturalist, "it has the heart
of an eagle and can surely be taught to fly."

After talking it over, the two men agreed
to find out whether this was possible.

Gently, the naturalist took the eagle in his arms and said,
"You belong to the sky and not to the earth.
Stretch forth your wings and fly."

The eagle, however, was confused.
She did not know who she really was.
Seeing the chickens eating their food,
she compulsively jumped down to be with them again.

Undismayed, the naturalist took the eagle on the following
day up on the roof of the house and urged her again, saying,
"You are an eagle, stretch forth your wings and fly."

But the eagle was afraid of the unknown and
jumped down once more for the chicken food.

On the third day, the naturalist rose early and took
the eagle out of the barnyard to a high mountain.
There he held the monarch of birds high above him
and encouraged her again, saying,
"You are an eagle. You belong to the sky as well as the Earth.
Stretch forth your wings now and fly."

Then the eagle began to tremble.
Slowly, she stretched her wings.

At last, with a triumphant cry, she soared into the heavens.

It may be that the eagle still remembers
the chickens with nostalgia.
It may even be that she occasionally revisits the barnyard,
but she has never returned to lead the life of a chicken.

In truth, you are an eagle with the potential to soar,
to be free, to experience your real essence.

But many people find they stay in the chicken yard
feeling safe because it's familiar,
but with no senseof purpose or direction.

Everyone has an eagle inside of them,
which they can access whenever they wish—often
with the help of an experienced eagle at first".

The Family Afterwards

Once I began my journey of recovery, I desperately wanted my wife at the time to join me and find her own path to healing.

I could see—just as she herself acknowledged—that she was in deep emotional pain. I knew she would benefit from support, just as I had.

Her pain was, of course, intensified by the fact that I had begun taking steps to "clear the wreckage of my past," while she had not. We are all vibrational beings, and as my own energy shifted so dramatically through the inner work I was doing, it created a profound misalignment between us. This misalignment wasn't just emotional—it manifested physically for her as well.

I knew I couldn't force her to walk this path with me, nor did I wish to. But I prayed she would find her own way to healing—not just for our marriage, but for her own well-being. I truly believed that if she found the right support, it could help us mend the fractures in our relationship.

That period was incredibly difficult for our whole family. The transformation I had undergone was so drastic that it was hard for my wife—and even my children—to fully accept. To them, my focus on sobriety felt like I was pulling away rather than coming closer.

During this time, I was introduced to a powerful book by *Melody Beattie* called *The Language of Letting Go*. It contained 365 daily meditations, but one reading in particular— February 12th—brought me to tears every time I heard it, whether read by the group or in my own quiet moments.

That passage spoke directly to my heart. I was being accused of selfishness—of making my sobriety the sole focus of my life. But deep down, I knew I had no choice. I had to heal myself first before I could truly help anyone else, even my beloved family.

That reading became my lifeline—a reminder that prioritising my recovery wasn't an act of selfishness, but a necessary step toward becoming the person I was meant to be.

10

The Language of Letting Go

February 12th

by Melody Beattie

"Letting Go of Those Not in Recovery"

"We can go forward with our life and recoveries,
even though someone we love is not yet recovering.

Picture a bridge. On one side of the bridge it is cold and dark.
We stood there with others in the cold and darkness,

doubled over in pain. Some of us developed an eating disorder to cope with the pain. Some drank; some used other drugs. Some of us lost control of our sexual behaviour. Some of us obsessively focused on addicted people's pain to distract us from our own pain. Many of us did both: we developed an addictive behaviour, and distracted ourselves by focusing on other addicted people.

We did not know there was a bridge. We thought we were trapped on a cliff. Then, some of us got lucky. Our eyes opened, by the Grace of God, because it was time. We saw the bridge. People told us what was on the other side: warmth, light, and healing from our pain. We could barely glimpse or imagine this, but we decided to start the trek across the bridge anyway.

We tried to convince the people around us on the cliff that there was a bridge to a better place, but they wouldn't listen. They couldn't see it; they couldn't believe. They were not ready for the journey.

We decided to go alone, because we believed, and because people on the other side were cheering us onward. The closer we got to the other side, the more we could see, and feel, that what we had been promised was real. There was light, warmth, healing, and love. The other side was a better place.

But now, there is a bridge between us and those on the other side. Sometimes, we may be tempted to go back and drag them over with us, but it cannot be done. No one can be dragged or forced across this bridge. Each person must go at his or her own choice, when the time is right. Some will come;

some will stay on the other side. The choice is not ours.
We can love them. We can wave to them.
We can holler back and forth. We can cheer them on,
as others have cheered and encouraged us.
But we cannot make them come over with us.

If our time has come to cross the bridge,
or if we have already crossed and are standing
in the light and warmth, we do not have to feel guilty.
It is where we are meant to be. We do not have to go back
to the dark cliff because another's time has not yet come.
The best thing we can do is stay in the light,
because it reassures others that there is a better place.
And if others ever do decide to cross the bridge,
we will be there to cheer them on.

Today, I will move forward with my life,
despite what others are doing or not doing.
I will know it is my right to cross the bridge to a better life,
even if I must leave others behind to do that.
I will not feel guilty; I will not feel ashamed.
I know that where I am now is a better
place and where I'm meant to be."

Thankfully, my former wife and I are now very good friends. Linnet has found a wonderful new partner, Neil, and together with my wife, Annie, the four of us enjoy an amazing relationship and share family gatherings with ease. If ever there was proof of the Course's message, 'With God, all things are possible,' this is it.

Uncovering the Fear

When I came out of the treatment center, I was amazed at just how much fear I had been carrying. That fear had always been there, but I had masked it with alcohol. Now that I was sober, it surfaced, and suddenly, I felt terrified of everything.

My entire journey became about uncovering those fears and releasing them, one by one. It's an ongoing process—peeling back the layers, letting go, and stepping into who I truly am.

In the beginning, I thought I was searching for a concept of a God which was outside of me. But over time, I came to believe that what many people call God isn't something outside of us—it's within us. Not separate, but present in each and every one of us.

I found this piece profoundly compelling.

11

I Asked God

"I asked God to send me his friends. He sent you.
I asked God to take away my pain. God said,
No, it is not for me to take away, but for you to give it up.
I asked God to make my handicapped child whole.
God said, No, his spirit was whole. His body is only temporary.
I asked God to grant me patience. God said, No. Patience
is a byproduct of tribulations. It isn't granted. It's earned.
I asked God to give me happiness. God said,
No. I give you blessings. Happiness is up to you.
I asked God to spare me pain. God said,
No. Suffering draws you apart from worldly
cares and brings you closer to me.
I asked God to make my spirit grow. God said,
No. You must grow on your own,
but I will prune you to make you fruitful.
I asked for all things that I might enjoy life. God said,
No. I will give you life so that you may enjoy all things.
I asked God to help me love all others as much as he loves me.
God said, Ah, finally you realize why you were born."

Everyone comes into your life for a reason, some for a season, and some for a lifetime

This simple yet profound idea helped me make sense of the comings and goings of people in my life.

At first, I often felt guilty when people left, wondering if it was my fault or if something had gone wrong. But over time, I came to understand that different people fit into different categories—and that was perfectly okay.

When two people have learned whatever lessons they had come together to learn, it's very possible that they disconnect in order to continue their learning process.

One person who has undoubtedly been in my life for a lifetime is my dear friend, *Gerry Gray*. Even though we haven't seen each other for years, he and his family remain deeply in my heart.

I first met Gerry in Nigeria when I took on my first shore-based job as a manager, after spending years at sea as a captain. It was a challenging transition—stepping off the deck and into an office, learning to navigate an entirely new professional and personal environment.

Gerry, an Irishman managing a competing company, and I instantly clicked. Even though we were technically rivals, he showed me great kindness, generosity, and guidance. In those early days, he even lent me spare ship parts when I didn't have what I needed—an act of support I've always remembered.

Years later, after we had both moved on from Nigeria, I reconnected with Gerry, his wife Joyce, and their two children, Jonathan and Zoe. I introduced their family to *The Hoffman Process*, the profound healing course I mention later in this book. This incredible program has helped thousands of people worldwide, including myself and my own family. Many well known Hollywood stars and even members of the extended family of the British monarchy have also experienced it's powerful healing powers and have had the courage to share their experiences publicly.

That reconnection also gave Gerry and me the opportunity to explore spiritual matters together. We even attended a hypnotherapy training course, deepening our understanding of the subconscious mind and personal transformation.

One day, during the course, Gerry shared a prayer with me. It had come to him in a moment of clarity, and I found it deeply meaningful.

12

A Friend's Prayer

by Gerry Gray

"Today, in harmony with loving, universal energy,
I will strive to judge nothing that comes to pass,
as there is neither right nor wrong,
only the perfect consequences of free human choice.
To give energy to those who address me,
for they are the source of my inspiration.
To observe my emotions and inner feelings and
to let them guide me in my alignment with my soul.
To stop and admire the natural beauty that is everywhere,
for this is the most obvious evidence of a perfect creation.
To meditate for inner peace and calm, for only through
these can I be fully receptive to Divine Guidance.
To listen intently to all who speak to me, for their every
expression contains a message I should not miss.
To trust and to love, for these are fundamental to life itself
and provide the way forward for my continued development.
Amen."

Understanding the Power of Acknowledging that I know nothing

The thing that truly surprised me when I came out of treatment was just how little I actually knew.

I had spent my life believing I was always learning—and in many ways, I was. But now my beliefs, my thoughts, and my entire worldview were being profoundly challenged—not just by what I read, but by what I experienced.

I came to understand that life itself is a continuous journey of lessons, always unfolding.

This next piece resonated deeply with me.

13

Life's Lessons

by Jorge Luis Borges

"After a while, you learn the subtle difference
between holding a hand and chaining a soul,
and you learn that love doesn't mean leaning,
and company doesn't mean security.

And you begin to learn that kisses aren't contracts,
and presents aren't promises.

And you begin to accept defeats with your head up
and your eyes ahead, with the grace of
a woman or man, not the grief of a child.

And you learn to build all your roads on today,
because tomorrow's ground is too uncertain for plans,
and futures have a way of falling down in mid-flight.

After a while, you learn that even
sunshine burns if you ask too much.

So you plant your own garden and decorate your own soul
instead of waiting for someone to bring you flowers.

And you learn that you really can endure,
that you really are strong, and you really do have worth.

And you learn.

And you learn.

With every failure, you learn".

The Power of Hugging

One of the things I was introduced to in treatment was the art of hugging. Before that, I had been absolutely terrified of it.

I remember visiting the United States for the first time and feeling awkward about how natural and common hugging seemed to be there. Whenever someone tried to hug me, I felt like a brick wall—rigid, uncomfortable, unsure how to respond.

Then, during my time in the treatment center, everything changed. Each morning, after we got up and showered, we would gather in a small group in the chapel. We would talk about how our night had been, discuss our dreams, read something inspiring, meditate—and then, to close, we would all exchange hugs.

At first, it felt strange. But over time, I realised how much I had deprived myself of this simple, human act of connection—and, to my surprise, how much I actually loved it.

Later, I came across this wonderful piece about hugs.

14

Let's Hug Again

Author Unknown

"It's wondrous what a hug can do.
A hug can cheer you when you're blue.
*A hug can say, *I love you so.**
*Or, *Gee, I hate to see you go!**

Great to see you! Where have you been?
A hug can soothe a small child's pain
and bring a rainbow after rain.

The hug—there's just no doubt about it—
we scarcely could survive without it.

A hug delights and warms and charms.
It must be why God gave us arms.

Hugs are great for fathers and mothers,
sweet for sisters, swell for brothers,
and chances are, some favorite aunts
love them more than potted plants.

Kittens crave them. Puppies love them.
Heads of State are not above them.

A hug can break the language barrier
and make the dullest day seem merrier.

No store of them. The more you give,
the more there are of them.

So stretch those arms without delay
and give someone a hug today.

I'm sending you a hug today!".

Who Am I?

One of the books I was required to read while in treatment was *Why Am I Afraid to Tell You Who I Am?* By *John Powell.*

At the time, I didn't understand why I had been given this book. In fact, there were many things in treatment that didn't make sense to me at first. But looking back, I can see that the incredible people at the center knew exactly what they were doing.

Years later, I came across a piece that finally answered that question for me. It's called *Please Hear Me.*

15

Please Hear Me

by Charles C Finn

"Don't be fooled by me. Don't be fooled by the face I wear.
For I wear a mask. I wear a thousand masks,
masks that I'm afraid to take off, and none of them is me.
Pretending is an art that's second nature to me.
But don't be fooled. For God's sake, don't be fooled.

I give you the impression that I'm secure—that all
is sunny and unruffled in me, within as well as without.
That confidence is my name, and coolness is my game.
That the water is calm and that I'm in command,
and that I need no one.

But don't believe me. My surface may seem smooth,
but my surface is my mask, my ever-varying and
ever-concealing mask. Beneath lies no complacence.
Beneath dwells the real me—in confusion, in fear, in aloneness.

But I hide this. I panic at the thought of
my weakness, at the fear of being exposed.
That is why I frantically create a mask to hide behind—
a nonchalant, sophisticated facade to help me pretend.

Yet, such a glance of true understanding is precisely
my salvation. That is, if it is followed by acceptance,
if it is followed by love.

It is the only thing that can liberate me from myself,
from my own self-built prison walls,

from the barriers I have so painstakingly erected.
It is the only thing that will assure me of what I can't
assure myself of—that I am really worth something.

But I don't tell you this. I don't dare. I'm afraid.
I'm afraid your glance will not be followed by acceptance
and love. I'm afraid you will think less of me,
and your laughter will kill me.
I'm afraid that deep down, I'm nothing—that I'm just
no good—and that you will see this and reject me.

So I play my game, my desperate game, and my life
becomes a front. I dislike the superficial game
I'm playing, this phoney existence.
I'd really like to be genuine and spontaneous and me.
But you've got to help me.

You've got to hold out your hand, even though
that's the last thing I seem to want or need.
Only you can wipe away from my eyes the blank stare of
the breathing dead. Only you can bring me to aliveness.

Each time you are kind and gentle and encouraging,
each time you try to understand because you truly care,
my heart begins to grow wings. Very small wings.
Very feeble wings. But they are wings.

With your sensitivity and sympathy and your power
of understanding, you can breathe life into me.
I want you to know that. I want you to know how
important you are to me—how you can be
a creator of the person that is me.

If you choose to. It will not be easy for you. A long
conviction of worthlessness builds strong walls.

The nearer you approach me, the more blindly I may strike back. It's irrational, but despite what the books say, humans can be irrational. Sometimes I fight against the very thing I cry out for.

But I believe that love is stronger than walls, and in this lies my hope—my only hope.

Please, try to beat down these walls with firm hands, but also with gentle hands. For a child is very sensitive.

Who am I? You may wonder.
I'm someone you know very well, for I'm every man or woman you have ever met and ever will meet".

Continuing the search for this thing called 'God'

I continued searching for God—this concept of the Divine that I sensed deep within me but had yet to fully understand.

One thing I was sure of was that everyone must find their own path to God. I was deeply opposed to any teaching that claimed, "This is the way, and the only way."

During my exploration, I came across a powerful piece called *I Dreamt I Had an Interview with God.*

16

I Dreamt I Had an Interview with God

Author Unknown

"So you'd like to interview me?" God asked.
"If you have the time," I said.
God smiled. "My time is eternity.
What questions do you have in mind for me?"
"What surprises you most about humankind?"
I asked. God answered:
"That they get bored with childhood, they rush to
grow up, and then long to be children again.
That they lose their health to make money and
then lose their money to restore their health.
That by thinking anxiously about the future,
they forget the present—such that
they live in neither the present nor the future.
That they live as if they will never die,
and die as if they had never lived."
God's hand took mine, and we were silent for a while.
Then I asked, "As a parent, what are some of life's lessons
you want your children to learn?"
God replied with a smile:
"To learn that they cannot make anyone love them,
but they can learn to love themselves and be loved.
To learn that it is not good to compare themselves to others.
To learn that a rich person is not one who has the most,
but one who needs the least.
To learn that it only takes a few seconds to open profound

wounds in those we love, and years to heal them.
To learn to forgive by practicing forgiveness.
To learn that there are people who love them dearly but simply do not know how to express or show their feelings.
To learn that two people can look at the same thing and see it differently.
To learn that it is not always enough that they be forgiven by others, but that they must forgive themselves.
And to learn that I am here—always."

Ask and You'll Receive

One of the profound realisations during my awakening was truly understanding the concept of *"Ask and you will receive."* This biblical phrase, attributed to Jesus, had always been familiar to me, but its depth eluded me until I began paying attention to the signs that appeared after posing a question. As my mind cleared and I became more attuned to my feelings and intuition, I noticed these signs manifesting in my life.

A particularly striking example occurred two years into my sobriety. I had been attending Alcoholics Anonymous meetings regularly, living a new life, and distancing myself from my previous corrupt and illicit business ventures. One evening, at an AA convention, a woman invited me to dance. Instinctively, I declined, muttering a weak excuse about not feeling well. That night, lying in bed, I stared at the ceiling and questioned, "Why can't I get up on a dance floor without alcohol? What is stopping me?"

I didn't anticipate such a swift answer. The next morning, at college where I was studying therapeutic counselling, someone recommended a book titled *Healing the Child Within* by *Charles Whitfield*. Its brevity appealed to me, so I read it eagerly. By the end, I realised that my aversion to dancing stemmed from deep-seated guilt and shame—a wounded inner child carrying unresolved pain. Recognising this, my next question was, "Where can I go to heal this?"

The following day, another sign emerged. Someone handed me a magazine called *The South East London Connection*, a guide to various workshops and training in personal and spiritual development. As I browsed through it, an advertisement caught my eye: *"The Hoffman Process."*

Two aspects stood out. First, the Hoffman Institute's head office was in *Arundel*, a beautiful town in *West Sussex*—this was the very place I had fled to as a child when life with my alcoholic mother became unbearable. Something about its castle and its serene grounds had drawn me in back then, and now, it was reappearing in my healing journey. Second, the advertisement featured a testimonial from *John Bradshaw*, author of *Healing the Shame That Binds You*, a book I was reading at the time. He endorsed the Hoffman Process as "the greatest inner child healing workshop of its kind."

These felt like clear signs. Without hesitation, knowing nothing about the course and no one who had undertaken the course, I contacted the *Hoffman Institute* and enrolled, trusting my intuition that this was meant for me.

Early Childhood Programming

"Show me the boy at seven – and I will show you the man."

Aristotle

The Hoffman Process proved to be a pivotal moment in my journey. For two decades, I had harboured deep resentments toward my mother. Despite her passing 21 years earlier, I blamed her for many of my life's challenges. Through the program, I released all bitterness, resentment, and hurt, transforming my relationships with both my parents and other significant figures from my past.

One of the most profound realisations I had during the *Hoffman Process* was understanding how we often unconsciously adopt both the negative and positive behaviours of the parent with whom we have the most conflict. In my case, this was my mother. This phenomenon, known as the *Negative Love Syndrome*, suggests that we mimic these behaviours in an unconscious plea for love and acceptance, as if saying, "Look, I'm just like you; or I'm just the opposite of you (when we rebel and do the opposite) now will you love me?"

With the guidance of my insightful teacher, I delved into the reasons behind my excitement whenever my business partner proposed illicit activities. Despite being a strong- minded partner unafraid to disagree on various business matters, I found it impossible to oppose his illegal ideas and would insist on organising these ventures myself.

Together, we uncovered a memory from when I was seven years old. My mother would take me to *The Lanes* in *Brighton* when she was drunk and encourage me to steal items from shops while she distracted the shopkeepers with her captivating wartime stories. Once we were out of sight, she would shower me with love and praise, telling me how proud she was.

My teacher explained that, in those moments, a 'program' was embedded in my subconscious associating illegal acts with receiving love and approval. As children, we desperately seek our parents' affection, so this programming runs very deep. As an adult running a successful business, whenever my partner suggested illegal schemes, this unconscious memory resurfaced, leading me to seek his approval by agreeing to these dangerous activities.

This experience highlighted how much of our lives we operate from past memories deeply embedded in our subconscious minds. This part of our mind can be the most dangerous simply because it is out of our awareness. Just as the most dangerous part of an iceberg is the portion hidden beneath the water, our unconscious memories can steer us into perilous situations without our conscious realisation.

Another area of growth and learning I had experienced during *The Hoffman Process* was in understanding relationships.

Relationships had always been challenging for me, as they are for many. Having completed the course, I discovered a further powerful perspective on this subject from the work of *Seana McGee* and *Maurice Taylor*, authors of *The New Couple*. Their insights were revolutionary for me.

Each chapter introduces a basic principle such as chemistry, equality, and peacemaking, and through examples and powerful pointers, teaches you how to incorporate these natural relationship 'laws' into your own couple, so that you and your partner can transform your troubles into triumphs and your frustration into satisfaction.

Here's an excerpt from their book that I found profoundly impactful:

17

Relationships Explained from

'The New Couple – Why The Old Rules Don't Work and What Does'

by Seana McGee and Maurice Taylor

"Disappointed in your partner?

Despite what you may think,
this could actually be a great sign for both of you.

When we first fall in love, we see everything in brilliant
Technicolor. The endorphin levels are off the charts, and
we exist in an altered state—very similar to being on drugs.

We whisper sweet nothings, share our deepest thoughts, and experience a euphoric sense of connection. This state can last anywhere from a few weeks to a few years.

Then, inevitably, the "high" wears off, and the illusion fades. Suddenly, the partner we adored has habits and qualities that drive us mad. Old wounds resurface, and we realise that this "perfect" person is not giving us the unconditional love and care we expected. In response, we begin using tactics—blaming, shaming, withholding, criticizing—to try to coerce them into meeting our needs."

At this stage, many relationships face a critical juncture. Partners may either choose to separate, initiating the cycle anew with someone else, or one partner might acquiesce entirely, becoming the compliant "pleaser"—silently sacrificing their own needs to maintain harmony. This unspoken resentment can manifest in stress-related ailments, including heart disease and cancer.

However, an alternative path exists. If both partners are willing to seek assistance and confront their own wounds, they can navigate through the power struggle, emerging into a deeper, more fulfilling relationship. They come to understand that their partner isn't responsible for healing their wounds—only they can undertake that journey.

This endeavour demands courage and isn't for the faint-hearted. Many individuals might prefer to numb their dissatisfaction through overwork, alcohol, or other distractions. Yet, eventually, these diversions lose their potency, and the underlying truth persists.

The true journey lies in discovering the only love that can genuinely satisfy—the love we uncover within ourselves, which I perceive as Divine Love.

This realisation marked a pivotal moment in my comprehension of relationships and became the foundation of my first published work, *Miracle Relationships: A Path to Freedom and Joy*.

The Power of The Mind

As I delved deeper into the power of the mind and our capacity to shape our reality, I pursued a training in hypnotherapy and Neuro-Linguistic Programming (NLP). The notion that our thoughts and beliefs sculpt our experiences captivated me. This awareness led me to a compelling piece that encapsulates this profound insight.

18

Time

by Dave Clark

(Originally performed by *Sir Laurence Olivier*)

"Stand before me on the sign of infinity. All you of the earth.
With the granting of the law of provination comes
the application of change. I will give you the key, and with

this knowledge, please realise comes the responsibility of sharing it. I will show you the way it's very simple. Throughout the universe, there is order. In the movement of the planets, in nature and in the functioning of the human mind, a mind that is in its natural state of order is in harmony with the universe. And such a mind is timeless. Your life is an expression of your mind. You are the creator of your own universe. For as a human being, you are free to will whatever state of being you desire through the use of your thoughts and words, there is great power there. It can be a blessing or a curse. It's entirely up to you, for the quality of your life is brought about by the quality of your thinking. Think about that - thoughts produce actions. Look at what you're thinking. See the pettiness and the envy and the greed and the fear and all the other attitudes that cause you pain and discomfort. Realise that the one thing you have absolute control over is your attitude. See the effect that it has on those around you. For each life is linked to all life, and your words carry with them chain reactions like a stone that is thrown into a pond. If your thinking is in order, your words will flow directly from the heart, creating ripples of love. If you truly want to change your world, my friends, you must change your thinking. Reason is your greatest tool. It creates an atmosphere of understanding, which leads to caring, which is love. Choose your words with care. Go forth with love"

Finding My Real Home

One common sentiment expressed by members in *Alcoholics Anonymous (AA)* meetings is the feeling of not fitting in—of not being comfortable in one's own skin. This sense of disconnection seems prevalent among many in *AA*. Interestingly, I encountered similar feelings during my *Angel Therapy Practitioner* training with *Dr. Doreen Virtue*. Many participants, though not struggling with substance addiction, also expressed a sense of not belonging in the world.

This led me to deeply contemplate the nature of addiction and the concept of disease. It also made me reflect on why I titled my book *Addicts & Angels*. I began to consider that perhaps, when we are born into this world, we retain a clear memory of our true home beyond this earthly plane. Personally, I found life here incredibly challenging. Even as a young child, everything felt harsh—school, parents, the surrounding environment. I was often told I was too sensitive, leading me to internalise the belief that something was wrong with me.

It wasn't until I encountered the spiritual text *A Course in Miracles* that I began to realise my initial instincts might have been correct. Perhaps the reason I found the world so harsh was that I, and all of us still carry a memory of our real home—of Heaven. Life on earth felt foreign, and I struggled to adjust. Then I was introduced to alcohol, which temporarily numbed that feeling, taking away my fear of the world. For a time, it worked. But as an incredibly sensitive person, alcohol affected me more deeply than it might have affected others.

This was just a notion I had, but when I finally encountered *A Course in Miracles*, it answered many of my lingering questions.

For those unfamiliar, *A Course in Miracles* is a substantial, profound book dictated to a New York psychologist *Dr. Helen Schucman* over seven years, beginning in 1965. She described hearing the voice of Jesus, delivering messages intended to correct misunderstandings that had developed around his original teachings.

This experience was deeply challenging for *Dr. Schucman*. She was an atheist, a highly intellectual psychologist who did not believe in God or Jesus. The messages she received troubled her greatly. However, with the support of her colleague, *Dr. Bill Thetford*, she documented the words she heard, despite not fully understanding their meaning. Over seven years, she transcribed *A Course in Miracles*—a complete Text, Workbook for Students, and Manual for Teachers.

The story of how this book came to be is truly remarkable. Eventually published in three hardcover volumes in 1976, today it is all contained in a single book and millions of copies exist worldwide, translated into approximately fifteen languages, reaching people from all walks of life.

For me, *A Course in Miracles* made perfect sense. Its teachings resonated deeply, bringing clarity and peace to questions I had carried for so long. Now, I would like to share with you one of its lessons that brought me immense comfort and understanding as to why I had never felt 'at home' here on earth.

19

Excerpt from Lesson 182

I will be still an instant and go home.

"This world you seem to live in is not home to you.
And somewhere in your mind you know that this is true.
A memory of home keeps haunting you, as if there were
a place that called you to return, although you do not
recognise the voice, nor what it is the voice reminds you of.
Yet still you feel an alien here, from somewhere all unknown.
Nothing so definite that you could say with certainty
you are an exile here. Just a persistent feeling, sometimes not
more than a tiny throb, at other times hardly remembered,
actively dismissed, but surely to return to mind again.

No one but knows whereof we speak. Yet some try to put
by their suffering in games they play to occupy their time,
and keep their sadness from them. Others will deny that
they are sad, and do not recognise their tears at all.
Still others will maintain that what we speak of
is illusion, not to be considered more than but a dream.
Yet who, in simple honesty, without defensiveness and
self-deception, would deny he understands the words we speak?

We speak today for everyone who walks this world,
for he is not at home. He goes uncertainly about in

endless search, seeking in darkness what he cannot find; not recognising what it is he seeks. A thousand homes he makes, yet none contents his restless mind. He does not understand he builds in vain. The home he seeks cannot be made by him. There is no substitute for Heaven. All he ever made was hell".

That passage deeply resonated with me, encapsulating the profound realisation that this world isn't my true home. *A Course in Miracles* is both profound and challenging. While its essence is simple, its teachings can be difficult to grasp, as they challenge and overturn many of our conditioned beliefs about ourselves and the world. Despite these challenges, I found immense reassurance in its messages.

The core teaching of *A Course in Miracles* suggests that our physical world—everything we experience—is merely a dream, an illusion. Our true essence is Spiritual , not confined to this physical world. This concept is profound and often challenging to grasp, yet it forms the foundation of the Course's teachings.

One day, while *Helen Schucman* was working with her colleague *Bill Thetford*, reading aloud some of the dictated notes, she transcribed a passage that they later recognized as an alternative to the traditional Lord's Prayer. This beautiful piece has become a cherished part of my daily life; my wife, Annie, and I read it together every day.

This prayer, as presented in *A Course in Miracles*, offers a fresh perspective on the traditional Lord's Prayer, aligning with the Course's teachings on forgiveness and the illusory nature of our world.

20

From Chapter 16 of the Text of A Course in Miracles

"Forgive us our illusions, Father, and help us to accept our true relationship with You, in which there are no illusions, and where none can ever enter. Our holiness is Yours. What can there be in us that needs forgiveness when Yours is perfect? The sleep of forgetfulness is only the unwillingness to remember Your forgiveness and Your Love. Let us not wander into temptation, for the temptation of the Son of God is not Your Will. And let us receive only what You have given, and accept but this into the minds which You created and which You love. Amen."

When people ask me about *A Course in Miracles*, I often describe it as a profound journey into forgiveness—but not in the conventional sense. The Course introduces a deeper kind of forgiveness, one that goes beyond merely pardoning someone for a perceived wrongdoing. It invites us to see through the very illusion of wrongdoing itself. This form of forgiveness is about releasing all resentments, bitterness, and hurt—not just for the sake of others, but for our own peace and healing. As we heal, the entire world benefits.

The term "sin" originates from the Greek word "hamartia," which means "to miss the mark." In ancient times, this term was used in archery to describe an archer missing the target. Understanding sin as a "mistake" implies that it can be corrected and doesn't inherently demand punishment. However, when we perceive sin as a grievous offence, it often leads to feelings of guilt, which in turn create a cycle of shame and a perceived need for punishment. The consistent answer to any perceived 'problem' one encounters in the world of form is this special kind of forgiveness which the Course teaches.

To illustrate this concept, I'd like to share another passage from one of the Course's lessons.

21

Excerpt from Lesson 122 of
A Course in Miracles

Forgiveness offers everything I want.

"What could you want forgiveness cannot give?
Do you want peace? Forgiveness offers it.
Do you want happiness, a quiet mind, a certainty
of purpose, and a sense of worth and beauty that
transcends the world? Do you want care and safety,
and the warmth of sure protection always?
Do you want a quietness that cannot be disturbed,
a gentleness that never can be hurt, a deep abiding comfort,
and a rest so perfect it can never be upset?
All this forgiveness offers you, and more.

It sparkles on your eyes as you awake,
and gives you joy with which to meet the day.
It soothes your forehead while you sleep,
and rests upon your eyelids so you see
no dreams of fear and evil, malice and attack.
And when you wake again, it offers you
another day of happiness and peace.
All this forgiveness offers you, and more."

A Closing Reflection
A Message of Hope

I trust that as you've journeyed through these readings, you have found inspiration, comfort, and perhaps a deeper sense of connection to yourself and the world around you.

These words, these lessons, and these insights were not just stepping stones on my path—they were lifelines. They guided me through darkness, helped me find clarity, and ultimately led me to a place of healing and peace. My desire is that they do the same for you.

The greatest lesson I had to learn—and one that took me many years—was the importance of letting go of guilt. Guilt, in any form, serves no one. It does not serve you, and it does not serve the world. For much of my life, I carried the weight of past mistakes, believing on some level that I needed to suffer for them. But suffering does not heal—it only reinforces the illusion of separation from love, from joy, and from the truth of who we really are.

For me, *A Course in Miracles* was the key that unlocked my understanding of this. It taught me that we create our experiences from the inside out—that the guilt we hold within will shape the world we see around us. If we believe we have 'sinned', and are unworthy, we will attract experiences that confirm that belief. But when we choose to let go, to release the chains of guilt and step into our innocence, our entire reality shifts.

This realisation has transformed lives—not just mine, but countless others. Today, *A Course in Miracles* is being studied and practiced in prisons, helping people behind bars find a freedom greater than any physical release could provide. That is the power of this work. It is not about changing the past or changing the external world. It is about changing the way we see the external world including others and ourselves—and in doing so, we change our experiences.

And so, as you move forward, I offer you a reminder of something deeply important:

You are worthy.

You are innocent.

You are a brilliant and Holy Child of the Universe, of God, of Source—whatever name speaks to your heart.

The words we use don't matter as much as the truth behind them. What matters is that you remember your own Divine nature, your own inherent goodness. You were not born to suffer. You were born to live, to love, to create, to thrive and to experience joy.

When we embrace this truth—when we stop beating the drum of our past pain and mistakes and start playing the music of what we love, of what we truly desire—everything changes. The entire Universe begins to respond in ways beyond our wildest dreams. It happened for me, and I know it can happen for you.

So as you reach the end of this book, know that this is *not* the end—this is only the beginning. You have within you all that you need to create a life of meaning, of purpose, of profound joy.

I believe in you. I honour your journey. I thank you for allowing me to walk alongside you, even for just a little while.

Go forward in love, in Light, and in the knowledge that you are never alone.

With much love and appreciation,

John Campbell

PERSONAL JOURNALING

Gratitude Journaling

"Gratitude turns what we have into enough."

Gratitude Journaling

"Start each day with a thankful heart."

Gratitude Journaling

"Gratitude is the open door to abundance."

Gratitude Journaling

"What you focus on expands—focus on your blessings."

Gratitude Journaling

"Grateful thoughts create grateful lives."

Gratitude Journaling

"Happiness grows where gratitude flows."

Gratitude Journaling

"Appreciation is the highest form of prayer."

Gratitude Journaling

"Gratitude changes everything."

Gratitude Journaling

"Notice the little things—they are never little."

Gratitude Journaling

"Gratitude is the bridge to joy."

Gratitude Journaling

"Each moment holds a gift—look for it."

Gratitude Journaling

"Thankfulness is the soil in which joy thrives."

Gratitude Journaling

"The more you thank life, the more life gives you to thank."

Gratitude Journaling

"A grateful heart silences fear."

Gratitude Journaling

"In gratitude, we find peace."

Gratitude Journaling

"Gratitude is the melody of the soul."

Gratitude Journaling

"Be grateful for how far you've come."

Gratitude Journaling

"Gratitude is the memory of the heart."

Gratitude Journaling

"Count blessings, not burdens."

Gratitude Journaling

"Gratitude unlocks the fullness of life."

Forgiveness List (Self & Others)

"Forgiveness sets the prisoner free—and the prisoner is you."

Forgiveness List (Self & Others)

"Letting go is how we hold on to peace."

Forgiveness List (Self & Others)

"To forgive is to heal."

Forgiveness List (Self & Others)

"Forgiveness is the key to freedom."

Forgiveness List (Self & Others)

"What we forgive, we release."

Forgiveness List (Self & Others)

"Forgiveness is a gift you give yourself."

Forgiveness List (Self & Others)

"Release the past to reclaim your power."

Forgiveness List (Self & Others)

"Forgiveness is remembering without resentment."

Forgiveness List (Self & Others)

"When I forgive, I remember who I am."

Forgiveness List (Self & Others)

"Only love remains when forgiveness is complete."

Forgiveness List (Self & Others)

"Holding on to hurt is holding yourself back."

Forgiveness List (Self & Others)

"Forgive not because they deserve it, but because you do."

Forgiveness List (Self & Others)

"True strength is in forgiveness."

Forgiveness List (Self & Others)

"Forgiveness is how we begin again."

Forgiveness List (Self & Others)

"To forgive is divine—because it heals the soul."

Forgiveness List (Self & Others)

"I release others to be free, and I free myself."

Forgiveness List (Self & Others)

"In every act of forgiveness, love wins."

Forgiveness List (Self & Others)

"Forgiveness is a path, not a point."

Forgiveness List (Self & Others)

"Peace begins when judgment ends."

Forgiveness List (Self & Others)

"The holiest place is where an ancient hatred becomes a present love."

Unhelpful Beliefs to Release

"Not everything you believe is true."

Unhelpful Beliefs to Release

"Old beliefs are not your destiny."

Unhelpful Beliefs to Release

"Your past does not define your power."

Unhelpful Beliefs to Release

"Release what no longer serves your soul."

Unhelpful Beliefs to Release

"Let go to grow."

Unhelpful Beliefs to Release

"What you shed, you outgrow."

Unhelpful Beliefs to Release

"Your story can change today."

Unhelpful Beliefs to Release

"You are not your limiting beliefs."

Unhelpful Beliefs to Release

"The truth is stronger than your fear."

Unhelpful Beliefs to Release

"Beliefs can be rewritten—start with love."

Unhelpful Beliefs to Release

"Outdated thoughts can't guide your future."

Unhelpful Beliefs to Release

"You are more than what you've been told."

Unhelpful Beliefs to Release

"Fear is just a thought—release it."

Unhelpful Beliefs to Release

"The mind can heal when the heart leads."

Unhelpful Beliefs to Release

"Shedding false beliefs reveals true light."

Unhelpful Beliefs to Release

"Your thoughts are not the truth unless you believe them."

Unhelpful Beliefs to Release

"Say goodbye to the lie—and hello to your life."

Unhelpful Beliefs to Release

"Every belief is a choice—choose again."

Unhelpful Beliefs to Release

"Releasing is rising."

Unhelpful Beliefs to Release

"Old beliefs crumble when love speaks."

New Empowering Beliefs to Embrace

"I am worthy of love and joy."

New Empowering Beliefs to Embrace

"I choose peace over fear."

New Empowering Beliefs to Embrace

"I am enough—always have been."

New Empowering Beliefs to Embrace

"My future is brighter than my past."

New Empowering Beliefs to Embrace

"I am guided by truth and light."

New Empowering Beliefs to Embrace

"Every day, I become more of who I truly am."

New Empowering Beliefs to Embrace

"I trust the process of life."

New Empowering Beliefs to Embrace

"I am healing. I am growing. I am free."

New Empowering Beliefs to Embrace

"My power is in the present moment."

New Empowering Beliefs to Embrace

"I believe in my inner strength."

New Empowering Beliefs to Embrace

"Love leads, and I follow."

New Empowering Beliefs to Embrace

"I am open to miracles."

New Empowering Beliefs to Embrace

"I see the world through eyes of compassion."

New Empowering Beliefs to Embrace

"Each breath is a new beginning."

New Empowering Beliefs to Embrace

"I am safe, supported, and surrounded by grace."

New Empowering Beliefs to Embrace

"Everything is working together for my good."

New Empowering Beliefs to Embrace

"I deserve to feel whole."

New Empowering Beliefs to Embrace

"I embrace my true potential."

New Empowering Beliefs to Embrace

"My mind is clear, my heart is open."

New Empowering Beliefs to Embrace

"I walk forward in love, not fear."

Example:

Daily Affirmations

"Today, I choose love."

I am the creator of my life.
I am free from limitation.
I am a living expression of peace.
I am heading to my new reality.
I am becoming the change.
I am divinely supported in all that I do.
I am worthy of love, success and joy.
I am elevating my life with every thought.
I am limitless in what I can achieve.
I am inspired by my own growth.
I am overflowing with creative energy.
I am releasing fear and choosing faith.
I am guided by divine wisdom.

Daily Affirmations

"Today, I choose love."

Daily Affirmations

"I am a radiant light in this world."

Daily Affirmations

"I am exactly where I need to be."

Daily Affirmations

"I am grateful, grounded, and growing."

Daily Affirmations

"I rise above fear and embrace peace."

Daily Affirmations

"My heart is open to joy."

Daily Affirmations

"I breathe in courage and exhale doubt."

Daily Affirmations

"Today, I walk with grace."

Daily Affirmations

"My voice matters. My life matters."

Daily Affirmations

"I create my reality with loving thoughts."

Daily Affirmations

"I shine from within."

Daily Affirmations

"Each day is a fresh canvas."

Daily Affirmations

"I honor my journey."

Daily Affirmations

"Today, I let go and trust."

Daily Affirmations

"I radiate calm and confidence."

Daily Affirmations

"I am in alignment with my highest self."

Daily Affirmations

"Love flows through me, to me, and from me."

Daily Affirmations

"I am a magnet for peace."

Daily Affirmations

"I show up as my authentic self."

Daily Affirmations

"Today is a miracle—I live it fully."

Printed in Dunstable, United Kingdom

69229707R00107